Every Wreckage by Ian C. Willia[...]
that our society needs. I don't b[...]
which a man questions his childhood, fatherhood, and relationship
to others and the world in such a vulnerable way. That toxic
masculinity is "this double-edged sword [Williams is] grasping by
the blade" in each of these poems. I was blown away by his bravery
and the beauty of his poems on every single page.

—Shaindel Beers
author of *Secure Your Own Mask*,
finalist for the Oregon Book Award

Every Wreckage is a sly, haunting, relentless book of big beautiful
wounds: childhood violence, homesickness for the dead, the debris
of a man's history and more. It's a book full of bullets and feathers
and secrets all unearthed in the loneliest of spaces. And more than
these things, the poems—language haunts each page as Ian C.
Williams not only ruminates on the shadows of the past but brings
them into focus against the present day. What a gift this debut book
of poetry is.

—W. Todd Kaneko
author of *This Is How the Bone Sings*

With nineties color, potent language, and a gravitational pull to
the joyous awkwardness of childhood, Ian C. Williams takes us on
a memorable romp through the tears and hayloft leaps of memory.
Beautiful and moving.

—Paul J. Pastor
author of *Bower Lodge: Poems*

In *Every Wreckage,* Williams explores a glassine interior, a time capsule, where wounds, once held to the knife's edge, attach forgiveness
to memory. In states of griefless grief, love transcends, and it is "harder to tell what is snow and what is ash" as "the orphan and the oracle" lay in the same grave.

Galactic, these poems are blessings, possibilities, sanguine
cosmologies.

—Maureen Alsop
author of *Pyre*

Every Wreckage, Ian C. Williams's dazzling debut, is a much-needed testament to father- and brotherhood. Through his elegant, controlled sense of form and lyric, Williams positions the reader in thick gardened ground and sly domestic spaces. Cicadas, lukewarm coffee, and the grave cycle throughout the book, marking the territory that Williams has so carefully wrought. *Every Wreckage* investigates the violence that is so often present in male relationships. But it would be a mistake to say that this book is "about" toxic masculinity. Instead, imbued in every line is the argument that men can be tender and nurturing and warm. While "...every closed door / doesn't shut out the sounds of another kid / getting his breakfast kicked out of him," the heart of the book is located in moments such as a late-night ER trip with a pregnant wife and in washing nervous hands repeatedly in the sink. *Every Wreckage* marries Sylvia Plath's creeping underbelly of the domestic to Phil Levine's tender brotherhood of the working class. The speaker confesses many things: depression, culpability, loss. But each time the narrative teeters ... Williams pulls us back up again like a tidal wave of grace. A grace that matters. A grace that says, "Every pair of wings a reminder that we're alive, / that we're all only a flutter of feathers and birdsong."

—Remi Recchia
author of *Quicksand/Stargazing*

This tender collection of poetry sings with bittersweet birdsong. Williams is deft at sharing well-observed everyday details, not shying away from the realities of past and present complexities, like depression and loss. "We are a kaleidoscope / of fear and frustration—/ we are swallowing stars while scrambling / for anything solid." Williams opens up his life in words, "cataloguing every generosity / I've taken for granted," and draws his reader in with him as he laments, "The dishes are never done. / So here I am again, pouring over / this calamity of glass." I found myself moved again and again as I read, filled with awe as he concludes, "Everything. Everything. Everything is love." A beautiful book.

—Joann Renee Boswell
author of *Meta-Verse!: it's going to be interesting to see how yesterday goes*

Every Wreckage

Poems

by
Ian C. Williams

Every Wreckage

poems

©2024 by Ian C. Williams

Fernwood Press
Newberg, Oregon
www.fernwoodpress.com

Printed in the United States of America

Cover and page design: Mareesa Fawver Moss
Cover image: "Plate 21, Mocking Bird," John James Audubon
Author photo: Sarah Bailey Williams

ISBN 978-1-59498-122-7

for Bailey—
you make me better

Contents

I.

Home Is Where All Your Bones Are Buried

Among these mountains, it matters
how far back you can trace the switchback

trail of your bloodline. We measure family
by its place in the firmament, how deep

of an impression boot soles have pressed
in the dirt. How weathered a name is

on a headstone. We measure a legacy by the shape
of a young boy's hairline—*I know whose son you are.*

Whose grandson you are. It's not so strange for a stranger
to know more of your history than you ever will.

Everything I Left in the Embankment

I pilfered a nearly empty oatmeal canister
from the pantry and filled it with trinkets—
representations, I thought, of my small life

I might one day want reminded of.
Hot Wheels, Legos, lesser favorite
action figures—letters written to myself—

spun together and sealed with Scotch tape
before I laid it—like a secret—in the hill
behind my parents' house.

Airtight and secure, the time capsule
idled the earth until eventually
I stopped thinking about it.

But I neglected how the soil saturates
the soft walls of the cardboard, how the shallow
grave can't resist the certainty of rain.

This was before my hands hardened
with adulthood's responsibility, before my shoulders
stretched the seams of shirts I thought I'd never grow into.

This was before the other burials—
the nights set to condensing bad memories and covering
each with sod, laying down the postcards,

the photographs, the time spent,
and misspent breath. Yet with every shovelful,
I underestimate erosion. Like the remnants

of childhood's safekeeping, everything resurfaces.
I'm finding washed out paper particles under
the embankment's ivy. Plastics half-submerged in the dirt.

The Clubhouse

It was never a revolution, never a rebellion
against household expectations—
only two children supported

by chimney bricks, the intrepid stitch
of youth threading limbs together.
Three stories and we weren't afraid

of falling, afraid our feet could stumble
past gutters, afraid the neighbors
might notice two brothers alight the roof,

circle, before climbing inside again. We were only scared
our parents might hear bare feet over shingles,
        so we tiptoed.

We stood against the horizon of hundred-year-old
houses, holding on to the invulnerability given
by the distance to the ground.

In 1991

       my parents tried to buy the yellow house
on Pleasant Street, next door to your childhood home.

This was before the the fabric began to detach and sag
from their Dodge Caravan's ceiling like an afternoon's

gray clouds, wet and heavy after spring rains.
Before the summers that bloomed pungent with chlorine

as I pulled cicada shells from chain link fences, filling
buckets flush with the molted shells of their transformation—

the months I spent barefoot despite a catalog of bee stings
and lessons I never seemed to learn. Before we were born,

we were almost neighbors, almost inseparable, we almost
shared every big dream a small town could muster.

What a wonder this is. Our kite strings were this tangled
together even before our eyes ever opened.

When We Were Both Children

He clutched it like a cudgel when he bludgeoned
my kid brother. It pulsed past his knuckles

when punching the back of my neck,
and yet if it fragmented after the impact,

I didn't pick up the splinters, only watched them
dissolve by the summer's oleander, standing

openhanded and stunned, blood running past
my upper lip. And here, separated by years

and state lines, I wish I'd scooped up
those impetuous stones and hurtled one back.

Boys Will Be Boys: A Confession

I'm still composing distance by closing doors
        on childhood haunts, on a backyard's invisible
militaries, trips to and from thrift shops

in the back of his parents' station wagon, dirt
        scraped between my front teeth after his fist's collision,
the blood mixed with spit. I'm pressing down

how he wore control like a makeshift crown,
        like war paint—how he sleeved his forearms' riots as if
his confidence didn't stand on the backs

of every other kid beaten down. But every closed door
        doesn't shut out the sounds of another kid
getting his breakfast kicked out of him. Every

curtain drawn doesn't hinder another shrugged
        justification of boys just being boys.
After it all, what we label childhood rivalry,

what we label history, I deny its resonance.
        Even so, I let in the whispers, wet
with the yellow stench of want,

of not letting go of my own unforgiveness—
        this double-edged sword I'm grasping by the blade.
After all this time, after he's made amends

and shed his unholy shroud, which of us is still
        learning to loosen his fists and bury it? I'm out here again,
turning over the dirt. Let it rest. *Let it rest.*

The Bread. The Knife.

You are slicing a loaf of bread.
The knife will not slip.
But your thumb will.

And the knife never knows
the difference between
bread and flesh.

But isn't this what it means
to be human? To hold on
to a wound as if that will fix it?

Another Way to Think about Secrets

If you look behind the armchair—call it
       an heirloom—in the corner where dust covers
hardwoods as consistently as a child avoids
       household chores—if you examine the maroon
of its upholstery, midway from the floor,
       you will discover a tear—call it a puncture—no,
call it an exact, stamp-sized square
       dug into the embroidered fabric, where a child,
with the ingenuity of his youth, the fear
       of disappointing his parents, a butter knife
and the crinkle of wrappers from stolen
       candies, needed a place to bury the evidence.
Call it *subterfuge*. Call it *safekeeping*. Call it
       what you call creating a place where no one
would look for another ten years, much too late
       for punishments or apologies to matter.

Self-Portrait As Seam-Sewer

If you're careful, you can creep the point of a safety pin, painless,

   past your fingertip's topmost epidermis. You can press its edge

under the print of your identity almost as if it didn't exist.

   In the corner of your parents' second-story hallway with nothing

except a safety pin and the solitude of empty hours, you can slip it

   beneath the surface again, and again, and again until the skin craters

like moonscape. In all the indomitable wisdom of nine-years-old,

   I threaded that metal tooth as many millimeters beneath skin paling

as it separated from the rest, as it lifted, ghost-like, in saddle-stitched

   ridges. This exploration of touch, its curious hunger, pierced through

tender whorls with glint of steel, with metallic snarl puncturing the crust

   to strike, in a flinch or the clip of breath, the broiling hive of nerve.

If this were a howl in the distance, I didn't listen—that is—I persisted

   in pressing its point under my skin as if taunting its status as *safe*,

as if the nerves had settled just a little deeper beneath the surface,

   as if, with another attempt, the result would be different.

Not Even Robert Stack Could Figure Out
Why I'm Here, So You Can Quit Asking

Even now, if you check the Google Maps Street View,
you can see where the tires scrawled my signature

in the gravel and dirt on the corner of Vinegar Hill Road,
when, at seventeen, I panicked and plowed across

a lane of late afternoon traffic and into the sudden quiet
that suffocates after car horn and the grit of my own teeth.

Before my father hushes me into the passenger seat.
　　　　Before we drove home in silence.

As the earth has scratched its long, pink scars in my shins
with its thistles and bark, I have etched lines

among these hills. My name is engraved in its soil.
When I dug up my ankles and ripped my limbs from this place,

I left something behind. And too often
that something echoes after me. It tells me to come home.

When Summer Seemed Longer

and seasons further apart, we used to wander
behind C's parents' house, hours spent oblivious
to time and future expectations. We spiraled
mountain paths through creek and briar to slopes
where trees opened to field and two boys could dream
of superheroes, mythic histories, whatever future
might root in the earth ahead of us—who we might marry
and how we'd raise our kids, what jobs we'd have and where
to move when we were old enough.

And when we thought we'd hurl ourselves
from the hayloft into adventure and the bales below, C didn't
second guess the decision. Just miscounted the jump.
Just confused *on* and *after* the three-count. He watched me
launch myself from barn wood to sky and fall
just a bit faster—farther than anticipated.
He listened to the fury of snapped metatarsals
and carried me all the way back to the house.
But C didn't jump. Not this time.

He didn't jump for another ten years
when he drove his wife and newborn son
four days to California, when he uprooted
from mountainside and built something
for himself elsewhere.

Self-Portrait As the Second Son

Wrap my arms and soft of my neck
        in goatskin, the extent
        of my violence. Outfit me

with my brother's clothes, his sweat,
        the odor of the hunt—
        blood and bone and ash.

How long have I grasped after my brother's
        ankle? For how much longer?
        Between drought and harvest

I am neither son. Between the tectonic dark
        and the cataracts, I can be the eldest
        child in your blindness. I might

receive his intended blessing, rip his heel
        from its footing and claim, for a moment,
        his place in your heart.

What I Misunderstood When Captain Kirk
Double-Kicked Wyatt Earp

I pressed closed fists to carpet as I watched the bullets
rip a wooden wall to splinters. All smoke and ricochet—
all hate and lead teeth chewing through barrel and stale air,
passing through captain and crew—

affecting no one. The bullets, the crew is assured,
are not real. They are only illusions and can only reap
the illusion of death. That's the real danger.

The believing you're dead
when no real bullet has ever touched you.

And the captain was never scared. Deadshot confident
with the assurance 1968's future afforded and really,
what had changed between '68 and '99? Why couldn't I
launch myself through smoke and cordite

against anyone with grim vision and questionable intent?
Why couldn't I fight for my crew, my family,
my first officer, my *Enterprise*? After all,
the bullets were never real.

Velvet

From the start, I've been stepping
on honeybees, rusted nails, and getting
tetanus shots. I was one of those
disaster boys—accidentally ripping sinks
out of the walls—unstrapping my rollerblades
and watching the basement flood, wondering
how to fix it before my father could find out.
But all I do is talk about childhood.

All I do is dig through its cardboard
rummage-sale boxes to compile
its corduroy mistakes. If there's a crowd
in an elevator or waiting in the hallway,
their pressed shirts, their crossed arms,
their low voices a murmuring fog
around my shoulders—I become a child
again—waist high with thin arms, big eyes,
and no sense of direction. These days,
I find myself looking at the tundra
of my father's hands, his laugh lines
stretching like the furrows in his vegetable garden,
the plaid he's wearing in the old pictures.
And here I am, wearing my adulthood
like a deer's antler wears its velvet.

II.

You Want the Moon? I'll Throw a Lasso around It and Pull It Down

following the total lunar eclipse of the supermoon, September 27, 2015

Give us an open sky
of black silk and silver embroidery

and I will not hesitate
to twist the keys in the ignition

and turn out of the drive.
But tonight, for this eclipse,

the sky is a mess of clouds
and catalpas branches.

Even so, my wife and I are out
searching for you. You know

we're out here, hunched over
the steering wheel, trying to find somewhere

far enough away from light pollution
and shade trees. You know we're searching

and yet you conceal yourself.
You're more or less a pair of eyes

peering through a hedge of briars.
But please—understand this—

please know that I am not
out here after dark tonight

to chase after you. No,
I am chasing someone else,

the one next to me, the one leaning
out the passenger-side window,

blonde hair streaming in the wind, starry
eyes lifted, searching the night sky

if only to catch a better glimpse of you.
I will follow her for far longer

than this short evening, even if the clouds
weave together and we never get a clear view,

even if it means driving down every forgotten trail
and back road between here and the state line,

even if it means letting go
of everything else you overlook.

If You Asked Me How I Feel about
Household Responsibilities, I'd Tell You

The dishes are never done.
So here I am again, poring over
this calamity of glass, scraping
my fingertips against the grease

burned into pans I ignored
on the stovetop overnight.
I'm plunging my hands
into the scalding gray

of dishwater, skin reddening,
and all I can think is how these
hands are not my father's hands.
These are not the hands that

delivered mail after the riffs,
that dug up tree stumps
from the backyard, that repaired
the money pit of my childhood

home—the hands that raised me.
My hands don't have a child
to raise. I don't have a small life
to soothe back to sleep in the early

morning's lamplight. No terrified
midnight trips to the pediatrician.
No cribs or monitors or any of infancy's
accouterments. I think of this often—

half-light wishes sifting
just beyond the curtain.
I think of fatherhood with its fears—
but this is foolishness.

Ours is no home for a child,
this house without a nursery—without room
for one. We can't afford to start
a family. We don't have the money

for diapers, for daycare, for insurance.
Just this ache, this pale ring in the belly
of a tall glass that I can't explain,
can't reach, can't scrub away.

Young Fathers

The young fathers adjust their snapback caps.
They circle the room, rocking their blue-eyed babies
and bragging how fast, how fast, how fast

their children grow. They produce measuring tapes,
as if by sleight of hand. How quickly they grow.
The young fathers adjust their snapback caps.

They cuff their joggers at the ankle, philosophize about craft
beers in the corner. They're so proud, the young fathers,
bragging how fast, how fast, how fast

their lives have changed. *You will know someday*, they laugh
through carefully kept beards. *You will know when you have kids.*
The young fathers adjust their snapback caps

and watch their wives lull newborns for afternoon naps.
They grin and reiterate familial facts and statistics,
bragging how fast, how fast, how fast

they're working to bury their heritage.
How they will never turn into their own fathers.
The young fathers adjust their snapback caps,
bragging how fast, how fast, how fast.

Because Memory Isn't Forever

elegy for Yvonne

Since you died, nothing here has changed.
I'm still sitting in my house halfway
across the country, drinking lukewarm coffee
and not getting home often enough. I knew
the phone call was coming. I knew it
was encroaching like a cat in tall grass,
about as fast as when your memory faded away.
I expected it but I didn't expect this quiet.
When you lived, we barely spoke, existing
in the distances holiday meals afford.
You spoke to your son—my father—
and I left my lips pinned shut.
What did I have to say?

What is it called when we are asked to bury
the family we barely know and what is the name
for the grieving we do when grief doesn't
so much as tap against the glass? What is it called
when what we're grieving is grief's absence?
But here I am, cataloging every generosity
I've taken for granted. The afghan
you crocheted is draped over the sofa
and my dachshund has buried herself in it.
The matching pillows stay on the guest bed.

I've used the luggage you gave me more times
than I can count. As long as I can remember,
neither one of us was ever any good at talking
to each other, but when you were forgetting
everything else, you remembered
my face, my name.

What Good Is This Degree
If I Still Can't Spell Neccessary?

This morning, the alarm only throws
seven flares into the dark—

seven thumbtacks hulled into the drywall—
but I haven't rolled over.

Right now, the garbage truck screeches past the house
and I realize that I've forgotten

to take the bins to the street again.
If I could, I might cocoon myself in these bedsheets.

But there are errands to run,
dishes to wash, papers to grade.

I know the dogs need let out. The summer clothes
need packed back into storage. I am so tired.

I need to shower, to brush my teeth.
I need to choose what clothes to wear. I know.

I've Always Been a Sucker for a Good Pick Slide

This was when we spent summer camps at a distance,
distracted by girls as the green wing of June
filtered through the sugar maples above us;
when you had your friends and I had my loneliness;
and I confessed to you my addiction, hoping to borrow
some of the confidence carried in your grin—
when you forgot about me.

Years later, when you called me over to your car—
its leather mixing with your frosted breath,
the growl of guitars crawling from underneath
the hairline crack in your self-assurance—
and you unexpectedly expressed your regret after a breakup—
as if asking for forgiveness—as if you knew,
in two years, this woman would marry me—
I think we were almost friends.

It's not every day that I think about you,
but it's often enough. Often enough to notice your absence
from my life. Often enough to see that break
in the forest canopy where we could have been brothers—
that break that shares your outline.

Landscape with Mother and Diabetic Son

After the dark drive across town, lit only
by streetlamps and headlights, after my cold sweats,
after everything I put her through
in the dog days of my adolescence, my mother
sits by my hospital bed. And there I am—a pale shell—
all the conviction of seventeen and asleep, tied to an IV.
Even now I hardly recognize myself.

But she does—this woman who has always
found me out, who discovered the sugared veins
that first brought me to this emergency room,
who blames her own family history for this heritage
of blood vials, spent syringes and medical bills—
for this disease without a cure.

This woman who stood by my bedside
when I was a husk of sheets—a vomiting chrysalis.
Who stayed awake and begged God that I'd blow out
my matches and bury my kindling. This woman
I wore thin with the worry that swallows appetite
as I withdrew further into myself and blacked out
the floodlights with accusation.

Who waited as I wandered city streets without
warning, slamming back doors and marching
my sneakers to shreds, rejecting every word
of caution and helping my body destroy itself.

This woman who was chasing after her son
with every good morning, every reminder,
every skipped meal, every night of lost sleep
when she resolved to drive his silence
to the ER. Everything. Everything.
Everything is love.

You Remember This

Sometimes you want to sit across from your mother,
across her kitchen table and occupy the same space

as the dust cloud of white flour, the pie crusts,
the Vaseline glass, the vineyard in the wallpaper.

The scones—you know—are in the oven.
Maybe it's the homesickness. Maybe it's the ache

of growing up. But here you are, feeling small.
You confess, you didn't expect to feel this distance

so deeply. But the state lines dig into your skin
like socks at the end of the day.

When you were just a kid, slumped over, hopeless,
bent under childhood's unfairness and a backpack

stuffed with clothes, comic books, and the intent
to set sneakers to pavement—you remember this—

your mother knelt beside you on the tile,
palm cupped against your tearstains,   *I won't stop you*

from running away   but you know I'll miss you
if you go.   She folded your shoulders into her strength

and you cried out your clenched brow, your balled fists.
Here, after twenty more years, is it so different?

When I Was Born, My Umbilical Cord
Was Twice Wrapped around My Neck

so tight they couldn't slide a finger
behind it. Perhaps it's no wonder
I choke on my own words.

Self-Portrait as Bowerbird

Look here at this cathedral arch
I've wrought for us with beak and talon.
Look at this shelter I've culled

from castaway plastic. See?
I've painted its walls with berry juice. I've adorned
its grounds with every scrap of blue

I can find. So pour out your blue,
your reflection, your distance, your mountain ridge.
Scatter it from wherever you are

and give me the opposite of here—
the antithesis of this place. Here is only
brush, ash—loneliness.

The sort that aches like a fog heavy
over dead leaves and wizened fruit. Release
the blue of ocean, orchid, open sky. See how

I'm building this bower for you? See how
I'm begging you for its materials.

I Swore I Wouldn't Write Any More
Poems about Birds but Here We Are

Outside, my wife feeds the birds,
who watch from a safe distance and celebrate
as she offers up thistle seed, mealworms,
sugar water, suet. Her morning coffee
is lukewarm on the back porch.
Our new yard has been left untended
for years, grown over with thin trees
weaving through the fenceline, wild
and unkempt in their green youth, now full
with the constant chatter of sparrows and finches,
the shrill cries of jays and mockingbirds.

These are the treasures of new jobs, the comforts
of worrying less about dodging late notices,
of a home now large enough for a family.
We are reaching only for a simple life—
every pair of wings a reminder that we're alive,
that we're all only a flutter of feathers and birdsong.
This is the fledgeling work of thanksgiving.
With every blessing, every brush and hum
of realized possibility, we're out here again,
hanging bird feeders and spreading the seeds.

Upon Driving by Your Old House

Honestly, you might think I'd be tired of it. Of hoping
that somewhere in the narrow aisles of your fire hazard,

your bomb shelter, your immense paperweight of a house—
somewhere, I'm still a part of your life. And maybe I am.

Maybe I am tucked away in a spare room, wrapped
in paper towels, folded into a dated Ziploc bag and enclosed

in a tote with unread issues of *Women's World*. Mostly,
I just want to hear from you again. I just want you

to take a step out of your castle of brown paper grocery
bags, VHS tapes, televangelists—Grandmother, come out—

no one has poisoned the water lines. Can we go back
to when we talked and fed the geese in the park?

When you lived around the corner and I would rake your leaves
in the fall—before this grapevine twisted and convinced you

that my parents conspired against your health, before you left
and I had to learn forgiveness for what isn't even your fault.

How I Take My Coffee

It's summer and over breakfast—
the torn upholstery of the diner's booths,
the buffet lights flickering in the corner,
my French toast already drowned—
it's how we keep up, my father and I.

If I meet his eyes the right way, sometimes
in between expressions, I see it again—
that familiar glaze of concern reserved
for all the interventions to my adolescence.
That look when he followed me

to the attic and asked the questions I dreaded.
But there was always a question. Always—
you've been retreating up here. Or—your mother
found the poems you wrote and posted online. Or—
we're worried to find you hanging in a closet.

Or simply—*are you okay?* I don't know
if he ever believed any of my denials.
And now, across the table, I just pour another
cup of burnt coffee and tear the edges off
sugar packets. I can't make myself bring it up.

III.

Self-Portrait As Sin-Eater

*"a loafe of bread was brought out, and delivered to the
Sinne-eater over the corps . . . and sixpence in money, in
consideration whereof he tooke upon him . . . all the
Sinnes of the Defunct"*

                    —E. Sidney Hartland, 1892

Sometimes I catch myself   returning
to the forest where   thick in the underbrush I buried
my youth   its prayers   its bullets.

I had encapsulated   my violence, pushed back the soil
and dropped its fragments   foul seeds   into the earth,
dropped the shots I promised   God and myself   I'd never spend.

In that woods   I circled back   just in case
someone had seen me shovel   in the dirt, circled
back   to find it dug back up.

I catch myself returning   to find the corpse
of every pale wreckage I've worked against   my ambition,
set exquisite with gold   quartz

pomegranate   and just one place setting—
a sparrow   vivisected   feathers
spread across the plate   alongside a handful of bullets.

Under the shade   of a willow's dense sweat
I wept   swallowed small bones and bullets' lead
and hoped no one was there   to see it.

A Prayer Worn Thin By Moss,
   Lichen, and Repetition

Forgive me and let me
explain.   I've made a ritual
of withholding   prayers   like smoke
until they turn to ash
in my mouth.   It's easier
than setting up altars only
to dismantle them again.

There is no burnt sacrifice.   No fire.
There is only   the infinite.
Only a fetid offering   splayed in the dirt.   Only its roaches
and bot flies.   But You know this.

You've watched as I've divided the deepwood,
torn fern from burrow,   crushed the skulls, half-
buried,   mossy in the underbrush.   There is a risk
in knowing You can hear me in this wilderness.

If I give You my brokenness
its stale crusts,   its knucklebones
You may mend it. But isn't that the signature
of Your faithfulness?   Still You watch
and I keep pretending You aren't looking.

Incredible! If They Wanted To, There Are Billions of Spiders that Could Eat Us All Within the Year

My worries are taking shape
      and tamping down the grass
around my ankles. All matted fur.
      All urgency. All ferocious hunger,
they circle and swarm, chanting
      their half-language, their half-royalty,
their half-minefield.

They pour over each other,
      a hive of pileous fists—all jaw, fang,
hairless belly—boiling.
      I'm burning through the prairie,
lighting up the switchgrass—
      an orange tongue against chapped lips.
I'm not sure how much faster I can run.

They writhe, more tooth than skull now.
      More distended gut than haunch.
Even now, they multiply.
      Gamboling form over feral form,
their mouths are full of fruit—
      currents, tangerines, cranberries—
chewing bruised skin and salivating.

I May Be a Ghost, But I'm So Far from Holy

I hesitate the edge of every decision,
finding each heavy and silent,
which is to say, like finding
a gun at the bottom of a cereal box.
How can I not freeze, hands brandishing
the weight of this much responsibility
as I circle the kitchen's tile
without a clue, without direction,
with only the cold steel of countless
shots I'm unwilling to take? And once
it's out, the gun cannot go back
into the box, can't harbor its cardboard
waiting for someone else's confidence.
Even if I did press it back down
and bury it in the back of the pantry,
I won't be able to ignore it.
I can't begin to stomach its silence.

Screening Test

Over the past two weeks, how often
have you: Been feeling low in energy, slowed down?

> How often have I leaned away, a curve of spine
> seated on the edge of mattress, red-eyed and staring
> past the wallpaper? How often have I scraped
> fingernail against my wrist as if to shed
> my skin   or maybe   to pin it down—
> a beetle under glass   *For some of the time*

Been blaming yourself for things?

> *For most of the time* I have been bending back my finger
> and pointing a spear of blame at my ribcage
> *For most of the time*   I'm tattooing my legacy
> on the inside of my eyelids   that is to say
> is it really blame if it's responsibility   if it's truth
> if it's the pungent fruit I planted with every mistake
> I've ever made finally   ripened for harvest?

Had poor appetite?

> I don't want to swallow this fruit
> I don't want to swallow this fruit
> I don't want to swallow this fruit
> I don't want to swallow this fruit

Thought about or wanted to commit suicide?

> About the void   about the echo   about how easy
> it is to slide under the   sheets and stay there
> about pressing myself into the space between the drywall
> and the infinite   *For some of the time*   I'm wanting
> to walk out of the house   wanting to take back
> my words and bury them   to take and take
> and take what they call the coward's way out?
> *For some of the time*

These responses are consistent   consistent
consistent with   every single time I stood
in the backyard   out past the embankment and begged
God to take it   to take it and fix it or   to take me home
to let me curl against damp grass and sink deep
into the soil   *Please remember*

these results are not a diagnosis   but what they are
is enough   what they are is   recognition
a salt bath scouring   years of bile and regret
These results are common and help is available
These results are common and maybe this attempt
at covering their clarity is not enough   *These results*
are common and maybe acceptance is enough
These results are common and maybe asking
for help is enough.

Blight

Oh—you're back. And just when I thought
you had stolen out of the driveway.
I could have sworn I heard your mess
of keys twist in the ignition and the engine
sputter out the last of its sour despair.
And yet, here you are in my backyard—

O great bitumen slick—O half-prism
of the oil spill who roiled through my flowerbeds—
you grimace of grime and gravel that upturned
the hollyhock, who paved over the mulch
and stripped the clematis from its proper place
on the patio wall. Here you are, standing silent

in the gateway. So tell me something—this time,
what else are you after? What more can you take?

If You Let It Speak, It Says

Quiet down. Root your ankles in the heather
of your own skull. Even now, stay here.

It's better in this dark. It's better to spin these sheets
into a cocoon—no, into a hive even now. Stay here.

Gather up the termites, moths, and water beetles.
They are your neighbors even now. Stay here.

Keep your head in your hands. Pray only for small favors.
Anything more is a mouthful of fog. Even now, stay here.

You and me, we are one house. We are one throne room.
We are one throne—Ian—one voice even now. Stay here.

As Lazarus

How deep is deep enough
until I reach the bent rafters
of my own ribcage? I test
the extent of my dimensions. This—

this is an effort of pencil checks,
measuring tape, and desperation.
Behind this drywall of sternum,
I am certain that the same thing
that aches in the attic is what keeps
it standing. How far down is it?
That place I'm afraid to name.
That place where God lives.

I'm pressing up against the door—
an angry thumb against a tooth,
snapped loose in my mouth.
How long have I been straining
at the concrete slab of my own
foundations, barely making a scratch?
Again—again, I've been asking God
for permission to uproot my life
like a weed in the asphalt, to split
the stem of my spine and let me sleep.
And this is the miracle—again, again,
in a voice at once thunderous and still,
God keeps telling me *no*.

Compromises

I park the car in an empty field
               to bury my body double, to drop
               his mirrored limbs in the cistern

I hewed night after night. He kicks
               against the cords around his ankles.
               Hair over his eyes, he's singing

the songs I left buried in holes
               where the grass has already grown
               over. He wrestles his sleeves,

his hoodie-strings long like fractured
               concrete—the kind he wandered
               in the glow of cold afternoons

when wet palms clenched the fog
               in front of trembling lips, anxious
               arms pressing down old bones

beneath the clay of his chest. We
               are the gravediggers, our outlines
               syncing up to the backbreaking work

of erasure. I grip the splintering
               handle before shoveling in the dirt.
               As it falls, he wrestles harder.

The Dog

Outside the house, the same dog barks—
        spitting its tooth and urgency, its howl and conjured
        resentment, every night arced to the splinter

of moon and its own reflection. Sometimes
        it seems to slink off the lawn and get lost.
        But as soon as I begin to forget

its timbre, it crouches in the backyard
        and scratches at the French doors and whines.
        As with any dog,

it circles the house. It roots, nose first,
        through the flowerbeds, rolling its inky slick
        against the patio furniture, intent

upon establishing its scent as a fixture.
        It gnaws the table legs. Shreds the welcome mats.
        It has the biggest eyes.

As with any dog, once it's there,
        I can hardly chase it off. Into the dark. The void—
        its mosquito and roundworm. It's hard to chase away

what the heart wants when it wants
        to hold onto it so badly. Like a bloated memory,
        like a clenched fist, like a blood clot.

The Difference Between Fine and the Truth

Maybe I should roll back my sleeves,
stretch out my collar, open up my clenched fists.
As it is, I'm just collapsed on kitchen tile,
wrapping my fingers around the monuments of dust
where I've enshrined my brokenness. Even now,
I'm begging God to hold back the breeze.

Palms pressed to my chest, I'm extracting
my ribs, polishing and arranging them
into the silverware drawer. After all,
what is a knife? What is a spoon? A secret?
What is the consequence of this rote effort
at shielding my vulnerability?

If you knock, then maybe I should unlock the door,
invite you in, lead you past the piles of unopened envelopes
and baskets of dirty laundry. I should let you look
through the closets and search the kitchen cabinets—
this time, I'll open them for you. You can see it all.

Another Kind of Archeology

Once more, I'm repeating this ritual
of broom and dustpan, this exercise
in judgment—how much of this
baking powder can I salvage?
How do you tell what is powder
from what is glass? How can you tell
before the barefoot sting of finding out
too late? Now I'm stoking my frustration—
not at the cat, not even at the glass lodged
somewhere under my skin—just the consistent,
pale corpse of each past resentment
that lingers, that surfaces after every
ordinary irritation. But the baking powder
doesn't matter. The cat is fine. Only startled,
staring in moon-eyed silence from the hallway.
I'm learning that forgiving myself
isn't sweeping the floor. Isn't turning
the other cheek or some practice of erasure.
Sometime it's this excavation of needle and tweezers—
it's digging the invisible sliver of glass from my sole
and listening to the shards as it splinters.

The Opposite of Gravedigging

If I write a grave into a poem, the likelihood
is that I'll find a way to throw myself into it.
Too often I'm on the edge of an open mouth in the earth,
wrestling the sinew and bruise of my body-double.
Almost by instinct, I'll try to hook his ankle
and push him backwards to plunge, headlong,
a darkling meteor of dread and destruction.
But what if I didn't?

Every morning I return to the offering
I left in the night, the covenant I made with You to live.
I'm learning instead to catch my own wrist
and pull myself back from this precipice
slick with the sweat of years spent in conflict.
But is this chokehold so different from an embrace?
And if I can love that which is broken,
how can I believe that You can't?

As Job Sat in the Ash Heap

did he pretend he was somewhere else?
As for me, it's getting harder to tell
what is snow and what is ash,

which is to say that it's difficult to know
when the air is this still. From this distance,
the lines of the back lot and the horizon

become one line, an endless veil of white.
There's a windchime in the arbor,
but it hasn't stirred. Maybe I am dreaming.

But I swear I can almost hear a rustling
from under the snowdrift. I can almost see
a golden tongue of flame tremble behind my eyes.

Soon, the earth will erupt in orange, an endless swell
of poppies and marigolds and butterfly weed.
I could see daylilies and cosmos for miles,

a beautiful catastrophe of riotous bloom. From every
direction the hum and bustle of new leaves,
new blooms. Everything returns new.

IV.

What Do You Say We Bury All of This Archival Footage in the Back of the Garage?

Look at your hands.
      You're gathering again,

sweeping together all
      your damp and faded photographs.

Each load of soured laundry.
      Every cup of lukewarm coffee.

Slow down.
      Your hands are full—

How is this collection your history?
      Bruised fruit, dead moths, dirt?

You're gathering again.
      You're resuming this assembly

of skin and bones,
      syringes and splints.

Slow down. In twisting
      back the tape in this cassette,

you're missing things. That is,
      slipping things inside pockets.

Green moss. Damp soil.
      Pink and green antique glassware—

misguided dreams
      now shattered into infinitesimal stars

glittering through the forest
      canopy and overlooking every blessing.

What are you hiding?
      Where are you sliding these framed embroideries,

wooden mantelpieces, these late blooms
      and honeycombs? Where did you bury

the dandelion dreams of your childhood?
      Open your hands, Ian.

Open your hands.

Benediction

Bless this night,
its stars and its streetlights.
Bless its bedsheets, its pillows—
this quilt and every hour spent sleepless.
Beside me, she dreams.

Bless her steady breathing.
Bless everything she touches
and all she carries—these two heartbeats
bringing my world further into focus.
Let this moment slip from time's
closed grip and let me glory in it.

Seventeen Years

You always kept a jarful of cicada shells
on the edge of your bookcase.

You called it a conversation starter,
but it was just an excuse to elaborate

your entomological interests
and I was never one to mind—I still wouldn't.

Yesterday, I walked through
your neighborhood and wondered if you still lived

on the corner. If your parents still visited
without calling ahead or if the shed scrims

of salvaged cicadas escaped
their enclosure and carried you off as one of them.

Remembering the Details

There must be cocoons hidden between these walls—
Bear with me.   There must be moths hatching
and crawling and fluttering their dust through my closet.
They must be clutching collar and sleeve,

busy mandibles gnawing the threaded
heirlooms of my memory—a whole colony spinning
its silk   before emerging with intent
to devour every shred.   Hold on.

As I'm crashing through these walls of fabrics, hurtling
past stitch after stitch,   I'm finding more holes
in sweaters—here—in slacks, in suit jackets,
in every garment I've ever worn.

At Fourteen Weeks

This pregnancy finds us too often
in the emergency room.

And now the red flag of first blood
brings us back. We are a kaleidoscope
of fear and frustration—

we are swallowing stars while scrambling
for anything solid. The skies only grow darker.

Nothing ever happens at noon.
It's always a midnight drive beneath streetlights
that seem to know more than we do.

You're fatigued by the hour
and afraid you're overreacting—
I'm only grasping at my lack of answers.

How typical this is.

You are immersed in this miracle—
this gathering of microscopic constellations—

you are swirling together stardust
and all I can do is nurse my worry.

The Archers

No one who emerges from the forest is you,
        though many look like you.
But these men are archers—
        fingers to bowstrings,
they creep to the edge of trees.
        Their shoulders boil, glistening.

They're so focused on their own motion—
        oblivious to twig, vine, thorn—
they're passing across the underbrush,
        black hair—wet—slicked back
like helmets in the rain.
        Like gun metal.

But you're not one of these archers.
        You have already ripped your arrows
from the dirt and let them curve
        toward their target. I have already
stumbled away from the forest's canopy,
        already snapped the arrows' shafts.

Like the archers, I am watching the line
        of the horizon blur with the dawn.
Like the archers, I am still
        poised at the edge of a decision.
Like the archers, I'm not sure yet
        what I'm wanting from you.

Every night, the archers
        nock their arrows but never
release them. Every night,
        I'm watching the tree line.
I'm waiting for your outline
        to separate from the dark.

Call It What It Is

After I boil this carton of eggs, then I will sleep.
After the rolling boil smooths to a line, after I peel away

their shells, then I will call it what it is.
This attempt at forgiveness. But forgiveness

will not erase the kitchen. Not the house or the forest,
not the text messages or the state lines. Not what you did

or how I needed to rearrange this silverware drawer
of my chest afterwards. But I don't know how to define it.

As it is, I'm scared. Scared that forgiveness is just a flick
of the wrist holding the knob, a motion to turn down

the gas so low it's invisible. Only stench and suspicion—
never a full crown of flame. I promise—I won't strike

a match in this kitchen. But I've seen the contents
of your pockets. I know you have enough for both of us.

Where the Bells Went

When you tore through the orchard, arms outstretched
as if reaching for the low fruit—

as if the low fruit didn't surround your ankles
that late in the year—

you kept crying, crying
                where have the children gone?
                The ones who rang the bells
                Sunday after service—
                where have the children gone?
You kept crying, crying
                had I been more aware
                had I been listening when their songs
                slipped out of earshot, had I not
                looked away, their parents might sleep tonight.

Off in the forest,
in the high branches where the jarflies stay,

I swear I hear the bells, I swear
I hear the children singing.

Imagine Me and You Alone
Ordering Groceries for Delivery

Honestly, what comfort is there in eggs?
In meat and vegetables? Honestly.
All I want is carbs. In this isolate kitchen,
I keep checking, double-checking the boxes of insulin.

They're saying this fevered crown is an open church door
for a funeral. They're saying it's the gravedigger
for the orphan and the oracle.
With a newborn due in two weeks, what are of the odds
that this split tongue will slither
through the spaces in the window frame?

I'm washing my hands again. Rinsing groceries
in the kitchen sink. Where is the line
where caution crosses into obsession? Which step
into the wilderness twists a man's spine into an animal
running scared? They're saying that it's a matter of time.
That everyone will suck down this smoke.
This sallow ghost of suffocation and spite.
But I can't stomach this—
one step short of painting the doorframe red with blood.

Gun Adept

With this I am parsing sentences
on a whiteboard. With this I am
listening to students tell their stories.
With this, I am drawing sightlines
over desks, across lunchrooms. With this,
I am as much constructing a barricade
as I am my own undoing. Even now,
I am becoming a strategist, setting
a blockade of filing cabinets,

a crowd of desks piled against the door,
a belt cinched around its hinge,
a set of textbooks designated
for use as projectiles. In case.
I have placed a hammer next
to the window in order to break
its reinforced glass. I have instructed
everyone to jump—after all—
a broken leg is better.

My students will be writing anecdotes,
penciling in their thirteen years alive,
and I'll be pacing the aisles, as much
answering questions as asking
which one of them will stockpile
their rage and make that five and a half pound
trigger pull of a decision. Which one of them—
which of my broken boys—will ask me
to twist this fingertip of lead into his chest?

Ode to the Osmia Avosetta

O mason, you backwards bullet,
you careful builder, peeling back the color
from any nearby blossom and curling each around
your unborn children—how you bury them
and wait. How you leave them to dig through
your mortar of mud and spit—how they repeat it.

Small carpenter, enclose me in any chamber
you construct. I am watching you patch together each
perfect petal, every beautiful piece of each mistake.
I am watching as you collect basketfuls of color
to create a paper-mâché barricade of carnations
and chrysanthemums, amaryllises and indigoes.

Let me stay inside this kaleidoscope of bloom—let me
blanket myself in the brilliant scraps you leave behind.

It Wasn't until After I Pulled My Son from the Wreckage that I Realized I Couldn't Move My Wrist

I measure everything by how old he is now:
    onesies, sleepers, furniture, memories.
        I'm measuring how quickly cars collide

and the distance we overturn
    without a guardrail, how much dust
        the airbags jettison into the cabin.

How long can this silence
    last before his lungs catch
        the breath it takes to scream.

The dust floats in the bloated
    stillness, as suffocating as it is
        indeterminate. In this moment,

I am as much murderer as I am
    in mourning. As much father as vilomah.
        I am as much the grave as I am the gravedigger.

But he does scream.
    With everything he has,
        he reaches down into every minute

of his seventeen-month-old life
    and dredges up his panic and his will to live
        and never have I been so grateful to hear

the saw-toothed wail of his fear.
    Every shrieking decibel determined
        to be found and carried from this wreckage

of a car crunched up like a fist
    or an unexpected medical bill—
        and how I know his cry.

After the sirens and the smoke,
        after he calms in his mother's arms,
                she strokes his tousled hair and sings

You'll never know, Dear, how much
        I love you. He quiets, but I can still feel
                his scream radiate through my wrist,

now useless in the aftermath.
        Could this be how God responds when tragedy
                fills the ditches with our glass, tires, and steel?

In the silent smoke of calamity,
        perhaps the answer to our panicked prayer
                is the winnowing cry from the backseat.

When we nearly lose everything
        in the trench of own own miscalculation,
                how welcome is the grace of knowing

we all made it. Perhaps we cry out not because
        we're afraid or our lungs have filled with dust,
                but because we have a voice and still live to use it.

Slow, Slow

I need to write this down before it is too late,
before the soft curve of your arms
smooths into a boy's muscle,
before this red curl of flame covers
your forehead and fades to blonde,
The downeaster storm in your eyes is already
calming its waters and committing to one color.
You came to us so unprepared for this world

but already I'm bargaining for more time.
You're reaching for everything, for coffee cups,
for club crackers—for the future. Already your eyes
shimmer so bright, so round, always looking,
always finding new ways to grow up.

On Gratefulness

My son and I watch the rainwater
    fill the shallow pools in the pockmarked expression
of my weathered driveway.
    There, I've seen the rosy-jacketed house finches
find a spluttering bath in the concrete.
    To see the hard-set stubborn face stay,
as though sleeping, while little claws
    jig their way across it, continues to warm
the wrinkles settling in around my eyes.

Notes

"What I Misunderstood When Captain Kirk Double-Kicked Wyatt Earp" references the *Star Trek* episode, "Spectre of the Gun," which originally aired on NBC on October 25, 1968.

The title of "You Want the Moon? I'll Throw a Lasso Around It and Pull It Down" is a modified quote from Frank Capra's 1947 film, *It's a Wonderful Life*.

"You Want the Moon? I'll Throw a Lasso Around It and Pull It Down" would not have been possible without the work of Aimee Nezhukumatathil.

"Landscape with Mother and Diabetic Son" ends with a line after Lyn Emmanuel.

"You Remember This" was selected by Aimee Nezhukumatathil as a runner-up for the 2018 *Atticus Review* Poetry Contest. This poem was originally published online in 2018, but was republished in March, 2019 in the second annual print edition of *Atticus Review*.

The epigraph to "Self-Portrait as Sin-Eater" is taken from E. Sidney Hartland's article, "The Sin-Eater," which was originally published in *Folklore*, vol. 3, no. 2, in June 1892.

The structure of "Screening Test" is after Oliver De La Paz.

The title for "Gun Adept" borrows a phrase from President Donald J. Trump, who, following the Stoneman Douglas school shooting in February 2018, proposed that teachers with firearms experience should carry concealed guns in public schools.

"It Wasn't Until After I Pulled My Son from the Wreckage That I Realized I Couldn't Move My Wrist" includes a lyric from "You Are My Sunshine," first copyrighted by Jimmie Davis and Charles Mitchell in 1940.

Acknowledgments

Grateful acknowledgment is made to the editors, staff, and readers of the following journals and magazines, who first published versions of these poems, sometimes under different names:

Atticus Review "You Remember This"

Appalachian Heritage "The Clubhouse" and "On Gratitude"

The Briar Cliff Review "Velvet"

Crab Orchard Review "Boys Will Be Boys: A Confession"

EcoTheo Review "Self-Portrait as Sin-Eater" and "As Lazarus"

Fourteen Hills "Screening Test"

Ginosko Literary Journal "What I Could Have Been" and "Where the Bells Went"

Harpur Palate "Self-Portrait as Seam Sewer"

Kestrel: A Journal of Literature and Art "Gun Adept" and "When Summer Seemed Longer"

Moon City Review "Not Even Robert Stack Could Figure Out Why I'm Here, So You Can Quit Asking" and "I've Always Been a Sucker for a Good Pick Slide"

Salamander "Self-Portrait as Bowerbird"

The Ear "Call It What It Is"

The New Territory "Compromises" and "Self-Portrait as the Second Son"

Yes Poetry "What I Misunderstood When Captain Kirk Double-Kicked Wyatt Earp"

I am also immeasurably grateful to everyone who has taken time to spend with this collection: to Janine Joseph, Lisa Lewis, and Sarah Beth Childers for being an incredible graduate committee; to Chrissy Martin, Alex K. Hughes, Jenna Neece, Kaila Lancaster, and the many other readers who have given me feedback even when schedules were full; to the editors and staff at Fernwood Press that have worked to polish these poems to their current state; and to Eric Muhr who trusted this collection enough to select it.

I am further indebted to those who put me on this journey in the first place: to Donna J. Long, your belief in me has been transformative and this book wouldn't have been possible without your influence; to Elizabeth Savage, Maureen Alsop, Mary Rosen Kindred, Kevin McLellan, and all the other poets who have taken the time to help me improve my writing and become the poet I am now. Thank you.

My love goes out to my parents, Mike and Marcie Williams, who have loved me unconditionally and have built the groundwork for all of this work, and to my in-laws, Larry and Lora Deese, who have never ceased to support me through my endeavors.

My entire heart and wildest gratitude belongs forever to my wife, Bailey; you are my truest love and my most treasured companion. Without you, none of this would exist. Thank you so much for talking me through it and helping me dismantle and repair this collection until it could stand on its own. You are my best friend, and I love you.

Finally, I am utterly and eternally thankful to my God—O Galilean—for every blessing and intervention you have given me. I am always reminding myself that your love is higher than mine, and that forever is still too short a time to spend thanking you for it. You are my inspiration and salvation and without you, I couldn't be.

Ian C. Williams is a poet and teacher from Appalachia. He has earned a Masters in Fine Arts from Oklahoma State University and currently lives in West Virginia, with his wife and two sons.

Title Index

Y

First Line Index